For the Love of Horses

By

MaryAnn Myers

Sunrise Horse Farm
11872 Chillicothe Road
Chesterland, Ohio 44026
440-729-0930
www.sunrisehorsefarm.com

First Edition 10 9 8 7 6 5 4 3 2 1

Non-Fiction, Fiction, Horses, Racehorses, Equestrian

Sunrise
HORSE FARM

For the Love of Horses is an anthology of published articles written about the basics of horse ownership, commitment, and the love of horses. Along with practicality in every article, there is caring. MaryAnn Myers is an Equestrian Sports Writer and author of the Bestselling Winning Odds and Maple Dale Equestrian Series. She is an equestrian, horse trainer, and environmentalist, and lives on an organic farm in Northeast Ohio.

www.sunrisehorsefarm.com

Included in this anthology are original short stories, *Little Angel* and *Christmas Eve.* Enjoy!

"MaryAnn Myers writes about what she knows and loves. Horses."

Article Title List

A Horse's Loving Wish – Straight from the Heart
Horse Sense
Famous Horse Sayings - Fact or Fiction?
Blanketing Your Horse - Is it Necessary? Is it Wise?
Young Adult Equestrian Fiction
Beauty or the Beast? Cinderella or the Ugly Duckling?
Horse People Love Their Dogs - But Do They Belong at the stable?
Horse Vaccinations - Allergic Reactions
Summer Time - Fresh Water for Your Horse
Salt and Electrolytes - Who Needs Them?
Writing Adult Horse Fiction - Talking the Talk, Walking the Walk
Dust-Free Hay
A Naturally Clean Horse
Equine Mega Worming
Hay Nets - Good or Bad?
The Practice of Bleaching Water Buckets
Taking Memorable Photos of Your Horse
Boarding Stable Barn Etiquette
Safe Use of Crossties
Horse Whiskers
Stall Cleaning - Straw, Sawdust, Shavings and Pellets
Swine Flu Vaccination - Should We Be Concerned?
Horses: Bullies - They're Not Just on the Playground
Severe Weather Warning - Tornado Season
Little Angel
For the Love of Horses

Christmas Eve
Indigo Horses - Myth, Mystery, Magic
From the Boarding Stable to Your Back Yard - Bringing
Your Horse Home
Winter Water Buckets - Water; the Single Most Important
Nutrient in Your Horse's Life
Thoroughbred at the Track – Seven Days before the Race
Toothache, Sore Back, or Just Plain Misbehavin'?
Horse Whisperers and Those who talk a little Too Loud

A Horse's Loving Wish

Please.... Treat me with love. Treat me like a friend. Help me when I am in need, help me when I am afraid. Trust me when things appear grim. Trust me to know the way. I want only to please you, to carry you and to guide you, to travel through life with you. I nuzzle your face to let you know I care. I trot when you ask me to. I gallop like the breeze. Occasionally I limp. Allow me to rest. Bring the children to see me. Bring Grandma too. I know how to speak. My words are in my eyes. I lower my head so you will pet me. Love me.

I can count. I know the days you are not here. I listen when the barn door opens. I look. I wait. I have hay. I have water. I lower my head. I build hope again. Maybe tonight you will come, maybe tomorrow. I cough. I hurt. I cry. Love me, please. I jump. I soar. I graze. I whinny. The grass is green. The pond is cool and clean. I miss my pasture mate. He stands at my side no more. I nudge him. He does not move. I look for you. I need you to explain. Love me as I have loved you. I am frightened. My time is near.

I will not judge you. I live only for today. Brush me. Bath me. Blanket me from the cold. Shield me from the heat. Allow me to be me, and you to be true. Don't forget me. Don't abuse me. Don't mistreat me. Love me. Allow me to climb the hill with dignity. Be by my side when I lower my head for the last time. Brush the dirt from my eyes. Smooth my mane and straighten my legs. Stroke my neck. I am still here. I hear your voice. Love me as I have loved you. I nicker. Love me....

Horse Sense What the Horse Can't Say, but that you should Know

Let's talk about the practice of pulling a horse's mane. Okay, so maybe it's not supposed to hurt, the lack of nerve endings and all that, but it can certainly be annoying. A horse doesn't always distinguish the difference. We all know cutting hair doesn't hurt, a horse thinks we should stick to that.

Horses aren't faking when they spook. They don't think along those lines. If they spook, it's because something spooked them. Nothing in a horse's psyche can lead him or her to spook, just to get their way.

Fly bites. Some horses are tougher skinned than others, but all of them are in agreement, fly bites hurt. Thank heaven for skin that can be moved at will to dislodge a fly and tails to swat them with.

Flies around their eyes are particularly troublesome to horses, not to mention harmful. Do their eyes tear because of all the flies descending upon them, or are the flies congregating because of the tears and moisture in the eyes? A horse doesn't care about this who came first - the chicken or the egg, scenario. Flies "bug" them, period.

Do horses' have emotional feelings? Of course they do. Separate a pair that are "fond" of one another and find out. Look what happens when you wean a foal and mare. Get a horse angry and watch their reaction. Pet a happy horse and notice the look in their eyes. When their owner arrives at the barn and they nicker or whinny, if that's not all about feelings, then I don't know what is. Are you listening?

Famous Horse Sayings
Fact or Fiction?

You can lead a horse to water, but you can't make them drink? That's true. If a horse doesn't want to drink, outside of giving them an IV of liquids, it's not going to happen. Even if you squirt a syringe of water into their mouths, that doesn't mean they're going to swallow it.

Don't look a gift horse in the mouth. Do! It's not hard to imagine this saying's origin. Someone once upon a time was given a horse and that person blatantly looked at the horse's teeth to determine how old it was before accepting the gift. The giver apparently took offense, told the story, and now it's said all the time to imply ungratefulness.

Ridden hard and put away wet; this saying usually references someone not looking so good. Riding a horse hard and putting them away wet; not cooling them out, rubbing them down or currying them is not only poor horsemanship, it's a crime. It's mistreatment of an animal. Don't do it!

Sound as a bell of brass. A bell of brass makes a near perfect sound. This statement, largely used "across the waters" implies that the horse is perfectly sound. Imagine a lovely London accent and say it that way, "He's sound as a bell of brass."

Pee like a racehorse (I'm cleaning it up a little.) From the time a horse leaves the barn for a race and returns, winner or loser, that half hour to forty-five minutes is intense. When he returns to the barn he or she will have run their heart out, exerted an extreme amount of energy, got a little nervous here and there along the way, and will not only want and need a drink as soon as possible, they need to relieve themselves, NOW!

While some horses in the spit barn (the designated testing area if they win or place) take time to "go", it's not all that common and is attributed to any number of reasons. They might be nervous, new barn, new smells, new people. They might still be just a little too uptight or wound up from the race, literally and figuratively. Maybe they're shy. If the horse won't oblige after a reasonable amount of time, blood is drawn for testing. When that horse gets back to his or her own stall, they go. They go, and go, and go. "Spit Barn" – racetracks used to test saliva on the winners after a race, hence the name.

No hoof, no horse. True. So very true! Keep your horse's hooves healthy. Have them trimmed every six to eight weeks, depending on the weather. Horse's hooves don't grow as fast in the winter where there is cold climate. Be diligent. "An ounce of prevention is worth a pound of cure." That's not a horse saying, but it certainly applies! Clean your horse's hooves daily. Yes, daily!

Give 'em an inch, and they'll take a mile. This is a stretch, and the origin could very well have originated outside the horse scene. But if you a gallop a tough racehorse in the morning, and/or are trying to rate (pace) them during a race as part of racing strategy, give with the reins an inch, too soon, that horse is going to take off, and they'll be no stopping him or her till the race is over, which on the average, is a mile.

There are many, many more horse sayings. We all know what a "leg up" is. We all know the wisdom about not "putting the cart before the horse" or "closing the barn doors after the horses have gotten out." But the saying I love the most, is seen on bumper stickers everywhere. It simply states, "I Love my Horse!" It just doesn't get any better than that!

Blanketing Your Horse
Is it Necessary? Is it Wise?

For some horses, the answer is yes. It has become common practice to clip horses that are ridden in the winter months. Thus, they then will need to be blanketed. It's only fair since we have removed the coat given to them by Mother Nature. For them to be comfortable and stay warm, it must be replaced. I prefer a hunt clip, but that seems to have fallen by the wayside. Show horses are full body clipped nowadays more often than not.

Horse blankets have become big business. There are blankets for just about every size of horse and pony, and even for foals. There are blankets for every season and blankets of certain thickness and function within each season. Pick up a sale magazine from your local tack shop, and odds are there are at least ten pages of different styles and color, thicknesses and price. Choose wisely and accordingly.

As a rule, the average pleasure horse that is ridden lightly to moderately throughout the winter and stabled indoors at night does not need to be blanketed. There is no reason for it. He or she will have a nice winter coat, one that started in the fall and will stay will them till spring. It is custom made for them and they like it. Horses that are trail ridden throughout the winter, again, ridden lightly to moderately, do better if they are not clipped and allowed to have their own fashionable winter coat; one suited to their breed, temperament, physical conditioning, and age. It is that custom fit.

As horses age, they tend to get a heavier coat each winter. This is not just the Cushing's Disease horses, it is all horses. It's nature's way of taking care of them as they age.

Nature also has a way of putting an extra layer of hair on a horse going into the winter that doesn't have enough fat content. Fat is insulation. A plump horse will always fare better in a snow storm, so to speak, than his thin pasture mate.

Layer blankets as per the range of temperatures. It's better to add and remove layers than use a too heavy blanket that has the horse sweating underneath. For horses that are cold-backed, it makes sense to blanket them, but blanket wisely. If they are outside 24-7, they will need to be checked often. Check the straps for wear, check their back and shoulders. If the horse is sweating on a sunny winter day, he probably shouldn't have that particular blanket on in the first place. Waterproof blankets are great, but if they don't allow the horse's skin to breath, they do more harm than good. Blanket smart. Blanket safely.

Young Adult Equestrian Fiction

Teenagers love horses. They love to ride horses, they love to groom horses, and they love to read about horses. The horse books I read as a teen are still some of my favorites today. Horses have personalities and there are no two alike. It is the horse's personality that speaks to the young reader. The author can describe the horse perfectly, and it can be the most beautiful horse on earth. But unless that horse's personality engages the characters in the story, and thus the reader, it might just as well be a picture book.

If the horse has adversity to overcome, who better to relate than a teenager? Perhaps the horse is smaller than the other horses in the barn, or large and awkward, lacking grace. Maybe the horse is shy, scared. With practice and schooling, a horse can develop presence, confidence. With hard work, an equestrian and his or her horse can excel.

Don't think you can talk down to any teen fiction reader, or have a story that is too hokey. They aren't going to read it, not unless it's a homework assignment perhaps. And if it's going to have horses in it, then it had better sound especially true. Young Adult Equestrian Fiction is a genre in itself. These readers know the horse life. A lot of them are living it, dream about it, and aspire to it.

Be creative with your plot. The teenage character and/or characters in the story need to have issues, because issues are the way of life for most teenagers, and it's even better if the horses have issues, too. They develop a partnership with their horse, a friendship, they listen to one another. Be cautious about introducing a horse that's a rogue. Stories such as this were extremely popular years ago, but have a downside. While a rogue horse can be rehabilitated, it is rare that it will come at the hands of a novice. The teen might just end up getting hurt.

Young Adult Equestrian Fiction books make great Christmas gifts, so all the better if there is Christmas aspect in the story. The Horse Show scene is another popular setting. If the horse becomes injured as part of the plot, know that injury thoroughly. Make the rehabilitation believable. Thus said, be cautious about too much hardship in the story. Fiction, particularly Young Adult Equestrian Fiction, is an escape for teens. Give them someone to care about and cheer for. Give them, even if just for a little while, their very own horse. Let them ride like the wind.

Beauty or the Beast?
Cinderella or the Ugly Duckling?

Who doesn't want a pretty horse? I'm sure we all do to a certain extent. And granted, if the horse is to be a halter champion, then certainly beauty and perfect conformation is a priority. But as a general rule a horse's beauty should never be at the top of the list, particularly when it comes to a pleasure horse.

Personality should be foremost; more specifically, the horse's personality when relating to people, us humans. I won't single out any particular breed here, but the reality is there are certain breeds known for their exquisite beauty, and along with that, their challenging personalities. These horses can be very high strung and a little on the fickle side. They may like you one day and not so much the next.

I'm not implying that a not-so-pretty horse can't have these negative personality traits. They can. I'm only pointing out that when one goes out to buy or lease a horse, they should put beauty further down the list. The beast, could very well just look like a beast and have the heart and temperament of a gentle giant.

The big jug-headed too-high in the withers horse with an ugly coat, the proverbial Ugly Duckling, may just be underweight and lack muscle tone. It is amazing what a little tender loving care, good food and exercise can do to transform a horse. He or she may not ever be the halter champion in your state but that Ugly Duckling or Cinderella of a horse might just turn into a dashing swan or a beautiful princess in front of your very eyes.

Look at the horse completely. Look deep and not only see, but feel. What is that horse saying to you? What is their body language relating? Is he or she saying, trust me, love me, I will try my best to please you? Does he or she convey kindness, spirit, spunk, athleticism, whatever you desire? Does the horse have balance? Talent? What do your instincts say to you? He or she doesn't have to be the perfect horse; the most important aspect is that you want that horse to be *your* horse. Beauty will follow.

Horse People Love Their Dogs
But Do They Belong at the Boarding Stable?
Do They Belong at the Horse Show?

The question of dogs at the barn is a safety issue. Not just for the horses and the riders, but for the dogs themselves. The slightest thing can spook a horse and no two horses when frightened behave alike. Each is an individual and each will have a different reaction. Most horses can become desensitized to the presence of dogs. Some take longer than others. Some never get used to them. When the horse no longer feels threatened in any way by the dog, it will relax. Some even come to like dogs. Particularly the ones that do not chase them, bark at them, or come at them from seemingly out of nowhere.

If your dog is a barker, whether large or small, leave him or her at home. If your dog has a tendency to jump up and down and lunge, leave it at home. Use caution when walking your dog on a leash at the barn or show area. Be particularly careful with extra long or the extend-variety of leashes. Your dog might be the perfect little lady or gentleman, but can very easily become involved or entangled with a dog that is loose, or even worse, a horse on the loose.

I have been to horse shows where there are at least fifteen or twenty dogs present, without incident. I have been to barns where there are five or six dogs running free at any given time. I have also been to barns where dogs are prohibited, leashed or otherwise, and with reason. A child was bitten; a horse was chased into a pasture fence. A pony was nipped on the back leg by a playful puppy. The tiny puncture wound resulted in monumental vet bills and a long rehab period for the little Hackney. These things happen.

Use common sense. Don't tie a dog in the aisle way of the barn or a passageway for the horses. Don't feed your dog at the barn and not expect issues if other dogs are present. Don't place an aggressive or timid dog in a high-traffic area. Don't feed another person's dog treats without asking permission first.

Little dogs tend to spook a horse just as much as a large one. A sudden bark or a fleeting move from any sized canine is enough to unnerve even the calmest horse. Domesticated horses still have that fright-flight response. Out in the wild, a pack of dogs, coyotes, or wolves instill fear that has been passed down from generation to generation. Some horses will turn on a dog they perceive as threatening. Don't put your dog in that situation.

It's sad to think of your pet at home alone all day while you are at the barn or at a horse show. But think wisely. Take into account his or her behavior at the barn. Think of the riders doing their best to excel at the show. Think of the novice equestrian trying to learn to ride. If your dog is notorious for spooking horses or causing trouble, even if it is "just playing," leave it at home.

Horse Vaccinations
Allergic Reactions

My Morgan mare Malaki (cover photo) is allergic to just about everything; dust, wood oil, mold, mildew, corn, vaccinations. I used to think she was just a "special case" to put it mildly. But horses with allergies are commonplace. I don't know when the increased frequency of horse allergies all started or if allergies have plagued horses forever. I wonder if Roy Rogers' horse Trigger had allergies, or Dale Evans' Buttermilk? What about Man O' War? Or Seabiscuit? Exterminator? I wonder if they even had vaccinations back then.

Allergic symptoms to vaccinations vary in horses. Some will show localized swelling in the injection area. Some will break out in hives all over. Some will get rock-hard lumps that last for days and even weeks and be tender and sore. Some will go off their feed. Malaki falls into the "all of the above" category.

It's wise for owners of horses with mild to extreme allergies to have their veterinarian give their horse an antihistamine injection when they are vaccinated. In addition, I have found over the years that precisely where that injection is given, is equally as important as the injection itself.

Vaccinations on both sides of the neck with only one antihistamine injection given on one side of the neck didn't work for my extremely allergic mare. If the horse's neck swells as much as hers does and is that tender, they won't lower their head to graze or eat their hay. A hay net comes in handy under those circumstances for a short-term fix. But it makes more sense to try and do everything possible to avoid the problem of your horse's extreme vaccination discomfort. Shots in the hindquarters seemed the way to go, but again, only if the antihistamine is given in the same area. Vaccinations in the hindquarters and an antihistamine in the neck did not help at all in Malaki's case.

My recommendation, based on experience with this mare, is to have your veterinarian give the extremely allergic horse their required vaccinations in both hind quarters, and to have them split the antihistamine equally and administer it in close proximity to the vaccinations injection sites on both sides. That way even if your horse still experiences some soreness and tenderness, it's at least "behind their way of thinking, so to speak" and should not prevent them from lowering their head to graze and eat their hay. This practical application seems to work best.

If your horse shows signs of respiratory distress after being vaccinated, with or without an antihistamine, call your veterinarian immediately.

Summer Time
Fresh Water for Your Horse

When temperatures rise, the first thing horsemen and horsewomen most often do is hang an extra water bucket in their horse's stall. This is good practice, but only if careful attention is paid. A horse will usually have a preference water bucket and will drink from it almost exclusively and use the second bucket only when their favorite one is empty. Horses need fresh water and the glitch with that second water bucket is if it's full, it can very easily sit for days before it is dumped and freshened.

Worse, if it is only half full or slightly used and the person watering just keeps topping it off. It can go days or even weeks and not be completely fresh. The water will sour and by then the horse will only drink from that extra water bucket as a last resort.

Fresh cool water during hot summer days and nights is just about the kindest thing you can do for your horse. If they could talk they would agree. I'm not saying you are to run out to the barn five times a day to give your horse fresh water. I am suggesting you take every opportunity to freshen the water whenever possible. It there's only an inch or two of water left in the bucket when you go out to water, dump the bucket and start fresh.

Horses that dunk their hay or rinse their mouths when eating their grain need extra attention. Their water buckets won't take long at all in summer to sour. If you are in your barn at least three or four times a day, then one water bucket will probably do. If not, and the horses are only fed and watered twice a day, you need to hang that extra water bucket and keep both buckets filled with fresh water.

The same applies to water troughs. Keep them filled with clean water. When turning horses out at night, don't rely on the "dew" to water your horses. Make sure they have access to clean water at all times.

Salt and Electrolytes
Who Needs Them?

Most mixed feeds have salt included in their ingredients. But I like having a salt block in the stalls at all times anyway. Horses need free access to salt day and night. If a horse likes licking the salt from a salt block holder hanging in his stall, you'll know because it'll have the obvious lick marks.

That might sound a little too elementary, but it never ceases to astound me, even in big "high power" stables, how little regard is paid to that salt block after it has been installed: a great deal of them are just sitting there gathering dust and cobwebs. Pay attention. If you fed your horse and he didn't eat, you'd be concerned. Be concerned about the salt block. If the horse isn't using it, put it in their feed tub. They'll have to move it around to get to their feed, and will end up getting the additional salt that way. I am a firm believer that horses should have salt in their daily diets year round, not just in summer months.

I don't add electrolytes unless I have a horse that sweats a lot. It's at simple as that. Racehorses sweat during and after a race, they need electrolytes. Polo ponies do, too, and event horses. It's rare for a day-in and day-out pleasure horse to need them. If they do, follow the instructions.

Don't add more than needed. Watch for excessive sweating with horses out in the heat of day. A school horse that clods along during lesson after lesson, is less likely to need electrolytes than the horse that is "a handful" going over jumps for fifteen minutes or cross country at an accelerated pace. Be wise, know the horse. A horse that has been ridden hard, particularly on a hot summer day that doesn't sweat is cause for concern. Call your veterinarian and act quickly.

Writing Adult Horse Fiction
Talking the Talk, Walking the Walk

There are two popular schools of thought when it comes to writing fiction in general. One says an author should write about what they know. The other suggests you write about a subject you want to learn more about. I can't argue with either, except maybe when it comes to horse fiction. I don't think horses are a subject that can just be researched on paper and put into play in a story. The author needs to live it. He or she needs to actually experience horses to bring them to life. And I'm not just talking about standing on the rail at a racetrack and watching the horses gallop by. Sitting in the stands eavesdropping and taking notes at a horse show won't suffice either.

Common pitfalls for the non-horseperson writing about horses, is to use horse terms that are rarely, if ever, used by real-life horsemen and women. They may in fact be the correct terms. But for the everyday horse person, they end up getting in the way of the story. Using terms that don't apply to a certain horse group is another red flag of not-knowingness. For example, a stable of hunter-jumper horses will not be turned out in a corral. Yes, a corral is a corral, and any horse can be turned out in one, but in the real world, that hunter jumper is going to be turned out in a paddock. A racehorse wears blinkers, a buggy horse wears blinders. Imagine using one instead of the other in a story, where it doesn't belong.

The horse world is full of a wide range of characters, and while they each have different personalities and habits, they wouldn't lead a horse from the right side nor would they ever mount from the right side; not unless their lives depended on it. They wouldn't mount their horse and gallop off into the sunset either. They may have done that in cowboy movies, but it has no place in reality today. Nor could someone sneak into a barn in the early hours of the morning, tack two horses and leave the barn without a stir. Every other horse in that barn will/would be nickering and acting up. The sight or sound of that first person entering the barn in the morning means food. It's breakfast time.

In dialogue, the difference between sounding as if you know what you are talking about, might lie in the understated. If you know how to ride, it doesn't take a lot of explaining. Your characters' actions just become part of the story. The same with horse care. Don't make the mistake of naming every body part on the horse to prove you've done your homework. You and your characters need to think, live, and breathe horses to be a horseperson. And there are no shortcuts.

Dust-Free Hay

It goes without saying that you want to feed good hay, with little or no dust. That's a given. But it's rare to find totally 100% dust-free hay, simply because of the process of how hay grows and is baled. It's vegetation growing in dirt! Dry dirt is dust. It gets dustier if there has been a rain within a few days before bailing. It gets moldy if it rains just before and is too damp or got rained on after it was cut and lay in the field and was then baled. I can smell mold and mildew a mile away, I am allergic to it. But even if I wasn't, mold and mildew shows up in other ways.

If you pick up a flake or two of hay and it's heavier than the others, chances are it has mold in it. Sniff, (From an arm's distance if you're like me). If it smells musty, open it up and look. Mold is obvious and so is mildew. If it's even slightly iffy, don't feed it. Better safe than sorry. If hay has a significant amount of dust in it and does not smell musty or moldy, you can choose to soak it, hose it down, or return it. If it's just a light amount of dust, shake it out and wet it down. In a perfect world, all hay would be dust-free. This isn't a perfect world. If it were, all hay would be cut a week or so after a good rain; it would lay row after row curing in a sunny field for days before being baled. And it would smell like fresh green grass.

A Naturally Clean Horse

I am flat amazed at the mass selection of shampoos and conditioners on the market for horses. There are shelves and shelves of them at every tack shop and feed store. Horses have oil on their skin for a reason. A mild shampoo once every couple of weeks throughout the summer and a mild conditioner for their manes and tails will suffice. If you wash all their oils away, bathing them day in and day out until they are squeaky clean, you are paving the way for skin issues; dry skin, flaky skin, and sunburn. No problem, one might say, there are products on the market for every one of those conditions too, shelf after shelf and rows and rows of them. Hose your horse off between shampoos. Use plain water. It works, and chlorinated aside - depending on where you live, it's natural.

I know of a horse person whose horse started rubbing its tail morning, noon, and night. A pretty tail that would soon look straggly if this continued. Following the old adage that if a horse is rubbing its tail it needed wormed, he wormed it and the tail-rubbing continued. Turns out the horse was having a reaction to the conditioner he was putting on its tail, the same conditioner that started the problem and compounded when he kept using more and more of it to try and remedy the condition. When he rinsed it all off and left it off, the tail rubbing ceased.

Diligent grooming is by far the best way to keep your horse clean. Horses love being groomed and it's good for them. It's good for us. It's best to have a separate set of grooming supplies for each horse, but if that's not possible, wash your brushes routinely with a mild shampoo. Enough said. If there is a contagious skin condition rampant in your barn, follow your veterinarian's recommendations on how to eradicate it. I know of a very admirable horsewoman that puts all her brushes in a bucket once a week and soaks them in a little vinegar and hot water. On any given day you can pull up to her barn and see the brushes and combs drying on the fence posts in the sun.

Equine Mega Worming

We diligently worm our horses with the change of seasons. Some horses get wormed monthly, weekly, and even daily. Wormers are so common place; the cost of worming a horse is cheaper than having the old-fashioned fecal check done to see if your horse even has worms. Would we take an aspirin if we didn't have a headache? No. Then why are we treating our horses for a condition that they might possibly not even have? It is mind boggling that this mega-worming frenzy has become such common practice. Where does it end? Scientific speculation is that we are going to end up with super resistant, super worms. What will we do for our horses then?

Some boarding stables have strict rules about worming and the boarders are expected to comply. For stables where the horses are all turned out on the same pasture, this is a must according to the farm managers. They say you can't worm one horse unless you worm them all. I disagree. I think we need to get back to doing fecal checks on a routine basis. I think the fecal checks should be affordable. We need to re-establish a common-sense practice of only worming the horses that need wormed, and not medicate the others just because they happen to be in the vicinity.

To the horse persons lucky enough to have their own farms and their horses in the back yards, approaching this mega-worming issue becomes easier and I encourage you to talk to your veterinarians about worm management. As an added note here for those that farm organically, when you worm your horse or medicate them in any way, the subsequent resulting manure should not be composted. It is no longer a base for healthy, organic decomposition and future fertilization.

Hay Net? Good or Bad?

I used to love to look down the aisle of a barn and see hay nets hanging at the fronts of the stalls, horses lazily munching away. But I don't anymore. What was once thought of a healthy efficient way to feed your horses and save on bedding and hay in the long run since there was very little waste, is now considered unhealthy for your horse. Hay nets and permanent structured hay racks alike, are out. Studies have shown that horses inhale dust and hay particles when eating hay this way. They need to eat with their heads down. Hay on the ground is the healthiest route. It is the natural route.

Dust of any sort, whether it be hay dust, sawdust, manure dust, or just plain old dirt dust, is a major issue when it comes to your horse's health. You want to do everything you can to make sure he or she is not inhaling unhealthy amounts of it on a daily basis. Dust is inevitable, and ideally, you want a nice airy barn. In the event you need to use fans during the summer season, be careful where you place the fans. Fans on the floor stir up dust. Fans should be placed off the floor, if possible, preferably mounted on the stall fronts, with the cords out of the way of man and horse. Be careful when you sweep the aisle-ways. Wet them down lightly first and use a broom and light strokes. You don't have to get every last dust speck. Do not use a leaf blower. I shudder at the thought. There is a fine line between diligent and fanatic. Find it and don't walk that line.

The Practice of Bleaching Water Buckets

It's a great feeling when stalls have been cleaned and all the horses have been grained, hayed and watered. The halters are all hung outside the stalls, the aisles have been swept. It's a beautiful morning, not cold, not hot. It's just right. The birds are singing. No flies yet. There's an underlying antiseptic scent in the air. You take a breath and sigh. All is well with the world, at least inside your barn. You hope.

You've done everything you can to create a clean healthy atmosphere for your horses. But have you done too much? Are you guilty of over-kill? Horses are animals, remember. Yes we are, too, but that's the problem. We have placed our human standards onto the backs of our horses, and rumor has it we are not doing them the better for it.

When was it decided that we should routinely bleach our horses' water buckets? I'm not talking about using a brush and just cleaning them well. I'm referring to the practice of adding bleach to the cleaning water and scrubbing like crazy. I have seen horsemen so diligently cleaning their buckets; it looks like a bicep/triceps workout. Why? Because we think we're getting out the germs - horrible germs lurking in the water, for the very same animals that graze off the ground, where dirt, bugs, slugs and all sorts of "icky poo's" dwell. Water is different, I can hear the diligent horseperson say and I agree. Water in most barns these days, sadly, is chlorinated. And yet, with or without chlorine, water buckets still get scummy over time and smell. Thus said, I can swear on my horse's life, that I have never had scum so foul and so strong that a simple swishing with a brush could not alleviate it. So why, oh why are we scrubbing them to death with bleach?

A barn that has a contagious disease is one thing. I'm not downplaying conscientious attempts to irradiate that disease. I am referring to the caring horsemen and horsewomen who are exposing their horses to bleach residue imbedded in plastic and rubberized water buckets day in and day out, under the assumption that it is the right thing to do. It puts me in mind of the hand sanitizers that are so popular right now with our attempts to kill all contact bacteria, a practice which is now being touted as possibly paving the way for even stronger bacteria, the inevitable super bugs.

Give your horse's water bucket a good cleaning at least once a week and even more often than that. Clean it daily if you like; just don't use chlorine bleach unless chlorine bleach is actually called for. Simply dump your horse's water bucket and give it a swish with a brush and rinse. Horse's like fresh water. Make sure they have access to water at all times. Don't count on moisture in the grass when you turn them out on pasture. I shudder at practices like that and can't stress it enough. Give them water. Give them fresh water. Give them endless water. It is the single most important nourishment in their lives. They can live without a bleach-scrubbed water bucket. They cannot live without clean fresh water.

Taking Memorable Photos of Your Horse

It's all about perspective, an inventive eye, and affection. You arrive at the barn; you meticulously groom your horse. You spray him to make him look even shinier. You put his fancy halter on him, the one with his name engraved on it. You take him outside and you're oh so proud. You're ready to start clicking away. Then the trouble begins. He won't stand still. He doesn't like the feel of the leather halter; after all he doesn't wear it that often. He wants to graze. A fly is bothering him. He hears a noise. He wants to go back inside the barn. You start snapping photos anyway, thinking something's better than nothing. You position his feet repeatedly and he keeps moving them. He shakes his mane every-which-way and you have to comb it again. He turns his head to look at something and you miss the opportunity to take a gorgeous photo because you are still straightening his mane. He pushes you away. That would have been a good shot.

You can always call in a professional and if professional photos are what you want or need, that's what you should do. If not, here are some tips for taking great photographs. Don't expect your horse to pose. A beautiful photo is usually a candid shot. If your horse is short in stature, bend down and take the photo from the perspective of down below, angled up. Don't take photos looking head-on into your horse's face. Unless you're documenting face markings or something of the like, this photo, as the saying goes, "will not be pretty!" Your horse's face will look huge and the term jug head will come to mind. Have a prop on hand, one that won't spook your horse but simply interest him or her. Take photo after photo after photo. Even in a perfect world, on an average, only one out of twenty photographs might be one that you will want to frame.

Take the horse to the pasture and remove her halter. If she turns to run away, start snapping that camera - if she runs and runs, take some more. If she comes barreling up to the fence, nostrils wide and snorting, veins pumped, have that camera humming. When she runs out of energy and starts grazing, get down on the ground (safely) nearby, and document her every move. Zoom in, zoom out. When you've had your fill of those shots, stand far back and get her attention. Give her a command and see what she will do. The horse will most often pleasantly surprise you.

One of the best photos I recall is one where the horse was told to dance, and looked at its owner with the most incredulous expression. "You want me to what?" No, it did not dance; it had never even heard that command before. But its expression did make for an absolutely beautiful photograph. Another gorgeous photo that comes to mind was taken by a woman from the position of being on the horse's back. The horse had its head turned sideways; an ear pricked, and was looking at her, used to the sound of the camera snapping. Another was of a halterless horse who had his head and neck bowed, watching as someone picked out its hoof. In the photo, you only see the horse's face and his intent expression. Think candid. Think gorgeous! Think I love you. It'll show!

Boarding Stable Barn Etiquette

Each barn has its own personality, its very own unique feel. Some are friendlier than others. Some are fancy, while others are more down home. Some house very serious competitors, and there are those who just want to have fun. But across the board, the basics of barn behavior, barn etiquette if you will, is universal. When riding in an arena going the same direction as another horse, let the person ahead of you know if you are going to pass to the inside or the outside, say "inside" or "outside" and stick to it. Don't change your mind at the last second. The horse and rider in front of you needs to rely on you to make the right choice. It's hard to ride when you're looking over your shoulder.

When a horse is approaching you from the opposite direction, it's just like driving a car. That horse should most always be on your left. Changing directions and reversing should be announced also. You don't have to shout, just simply state the fact. Most often the other riders will oblige. Let them know if you are going to school over jumps. There is nothing more annoying, not to mention potentially dangerous, than having a horse and rider start taking jumps without advance warning. When entering and leaving the arena, say "Door" to let others know you are entering and leaving; approach crossties with regard to the horse and rider. Horses can spook for seemingly no reason at all, don't give them excuses.

Clean up after your horse in the grooming area and crossties. Until that bridle is on, there is no reason to not do it right then and there. If your horse is completely tacked, it's a given you're not going to unbridle him and put him back in a halter so you can clean up. Nor do you want to hook crossties to his bridle. Clean it up when you finish riding. Chances are if it is a busy barn, someone will go ahead and clean it up for you before grooming and tacking their horse. Thank them and remember to return the favor. A boarding stable with horse owners that look out for one another is the best barn to be in.

Thus said, this does not apply to giving treats to another person's horse. Do not, I repeat, do not assume it is okay to pass out carrots, apples, sugar cubes, low-cal treats, or anything of the like. It is not your right. Let me say that again. It is not your right. It is wrong. If you have asked the owner's permission and it has been granted, that's a different thing. Aside from that, even if the horse is the best beggar in the world and does handstands and somersaults for carrots, please, please, please, walk on by. That horse could be on a special diet, he could have just been wormed, treated with medication. He could be allergic. You don't know. His owner knows, and rightfully so. It's not your horse.

In certain barns, it's alright to give your horse extra hay. Not anyone else's, just yours. The best thing to do if you are finding that your horse doesn't have hay and you hate leaving him or her that way is to talk to the barn manager or owner. Ask them what time horses are hayed and how often, when is night check, when is water topped off? As a rule, horses are not always going to have hay in their stalls, particularly the easy keepers. They eat quickly and take a dream-filled nap in preparation for the next feeding.

If you do give your horse hay, be quiet about it. The other horses are bound to get stirred up when they see you blatantly serving up hay to your horse and not them. It is not acceptable in any barn that I know of to hay your horse and then go hay everyone else's because you feel bad, now that you have them all riled up. It goes back to not knowing each horse's needs. Again, check with the owner or barn manager. This applies even more so with grain.

Do not borrow another person's tack, blankets, and turnout sheets, fly masks; fly spray, etc. without asking. Do not borrow grooming supplies such as hoof picks and scissors without asking. Do not borrow grooming brushes and combs, period. It's not good practice. Don't leave your horse's halter hooked to the crosstie. Before you leave for the day, snap your horse's halter and lead shank together and hang it in the designated area by his or her stall. In case of emergency or fire, this step-saving measure could possibly save your horse's life. Post your contact information on the front of your horse's stall, including blacksmith and veterinarian's phone number. If you water your horse, rewind the hose. If you pick out your horse's stall, empty the muck basket and put the pitchfork away. Flush the toilet when you use it. Don't let things spoil in the refrigerator. Don't get into barn gossip, nothing good will come of it. Turn out the lights. Close the gates and doors. Be careful. Sound like home? It is your home; it's your second home. It's where your horse lives and chances are you spend a lot of time there. Enjoy!

Safe Use of Crossties

Standing your horse in crossties in the aisle way of the barn is great for grooming and tacking. It even works for blacksmith time. Most horses stand perfectly fine in crossties. They might fidget now and then, toss their head or paw. They might look around and try and socialize with a horse in a nearby stall. They might even "talk a little trash" of the nickering, whinnying kind if they get some interest. They may take a few steps forward, a few steps back. They might rest a leg, and be totally at ease with themselves and their situation. The ideal setup for crossties would be in a designated grooming area or stall that is open at the front. This would eliminate any distractions for the horse, and you. Whether it be in an aisle way or grooming stall, it is referred to as crossties. Where's your horse...? He's in the crossties.

The actual crossties themselves are first on the list for success and safety for you and horse. They must, and I cannot stress this enough, they must have quick-release snaps. Quick-release snaps are designed, appropriately, to release quickly. If your horse gets spooked from a sudden noise or action in or around the barn and reacts to the extreme, he may need to be "released quickly." My personal horse Malaki is notorious for becoming unglued when someone walks overhead in the hayloft. I can usually calm her, but having quick-release snaps has come in handy on more than one occasion.

The placement of the snaps is paramount. I have seen many configurations over the years and some are mind-boggling to say the least. I wonder why anyone would attach the quick-release snaps to the screw eye where the crossties connect to the wall. As a good rule, the screw eye should be high enough so that a horse rearing could not get its leg up over the crosstie. Thus said, if a horse does start rearing and manages to get a leg hung up, how on earth is the average height person going to reach up high enough to yank on the quick-release snap. This is no time to go searching for a stepstool or ladder.

Worse, I have seen crossties where the quick-release snaps are connected to the horse's halter. Again, if a horse is acting up and manages to get itself in trouble, what is the likelihood of your being able to get close enough to him or her and the halter, safely, to release the snap? For me, the ideal spot is in between. Have two lengths of crossties on each side, with the quick-release snap connecting them in between, preferably a little higher than midway. When your horse is in trouble, rearing, backing up in a fit, trying to bolt forward or sitting down from pulling back so hard, it's going to be the easiest route to your unsnapping the quick-release without you getting hurt. It's the safest route for the horse, too.

A truly fastidious person can have quick-release snaps at the top and midway. I have seen barns where the connection to the screw eyes on the wall is a small double or triple loop made out of baling twine. In the event your horse starts acting up excessively, the baling twine will snap and can easily be replaced once your horse is calmed down. The chances of your needing to pull the quick-release snaps are not as common as one might think. Usually some calm assurance if the horse gets upset is enough to settle him or her down. Sometimes a firm word or two, particularly if they are pulling back on the crossties, will do the trick. A simple, "Get up" in a low voice will work wonders most often.

For horses that have never stood in crossties before, take it slow. Ease them into it. Groom them in the aisle way on a lead shank. Get them used to the area and process. You might want to keep the lead shank on them the first time or two that you hook them up to the crossties. Put the cross ties on one side, and put some tension on the lead shank on the other. Have them step forward and back, to get the feel of being tethered on both sides. The next time you go to hook them up, they will be accustomed to the routine. As a word of caution, me being an old Thoroughbred racehorse trainer, Thoroughbreds acquired off the track know nothing of crossties. They have a single tie in their stalls, usually at the back or on the side, and that's where they are groomed. They are hand held for the blacksmith. Take it extra slow when introducing them to crossties. Don't assume anything with any breed of horse. If you purchase a new horse, ask if he or she is used to crossties. Don't find out the hard way. Again, safety is the key, for you, and for the horse.

Horse Whiskers

Cats have whiskers, dogs have whiskers. Cows have whiskers. Horses have whiskers. I'd venture to say most every animal on earth has whiskers. Whiskers seem to be the norm, a necessity. Why then do we clip our horse's whiskers? And are we doing them a disservice?

From all my research, extensive to say the least, I believe we are doing them a disservice. A horse having whiskers is a natural thing. They are feelers, necessary when grazing, when drinking water, when eating grain or hay, when nuzzling one another. Horses can't see what's down there at the end of their noses, they need feelers, hence the whiskers.

When you look at the evolution of the horse, how they have come to be the magnificent animals that they are, we see that their conformation and size has changed drastically. I think it's safe to say they had whiskers way back when, and they still have them now, so that should tell us something. The whiskers are there for a reason or they would have vanished by now.

I think the reason we clip, and I say "we" including me in the past tense, is because we think the horse looks prettier without them, grander. It's all about looks. I doubt anyone has set out to clip or shave their horse's whiskers to make him a healthier horse, to give them a simpler life, a better self image, to lighten the load, all of the above. It's all about looks! And unfortunately, the horse has no say in the matter. One way or another, be it clippers, scissors, or the ever-so-handy sensitive-skin disposable razors, those whiskers are falling by the wayside in the blink of an eye. Perhaps we should re-examine our need for the clean-shaven equine muzzle. Maybe, just maybe, we should listen to Mother Nature in this regard.

Stall Cleaning

Straw, Sawdust, Shavings and Pellets
Bedding Your Horse Down

My favorite stall bedding for horses is straw. This preference probably dates back to my old Thoroughbred racetrack days. I think cleaning a stall bed on straw is easy and efficient. Done properly, there is very little waste. You start by cleaning a corner first, pile the good straw there, and work your way around all four corners. Pick out any remaining manure and wet areas in the middle and then fluff the straw back around the stall. It's as simple as that. I think if a horse could have a say in the matter, they might like straw best, too. It's about as natural as can be to where they'd lie down if given the choice outside. I can imagine them looking out at a field of tall grass when thinking about taking a nap, and then looking back at a (hypothetical) field of sawdust. Hmmm... The sad thing about straw it that's it's almost as expensive as hay in most parts, and in certain areas of the country, it is almost double the price of hay. The demand for straw in landscaping is largely responsible for straw's high prices.

Sawdust is the most commonly-used bedding in stables. If one is lucky and has an ample storage area, they can get it hauled in by the dump- truck load, which is the most economical route. When buying bagged sawdust, I'd venture to say it costs just as much to bed your horse as it does to feed them. Sawdust has additional drawbacks. For one, as the name implies, it is dust. Dust is not good for a horse; the finer the sawdust the higher the risk of respiratory ills. You can dampen the sawdust once you bed the stall down, but the dampness can only be dampness (not wet) and the desired amount of moisture will soon evaporate. If you walk through your horse's stall and stir up dust, imagine the dust bowl your horse creates over the course of a day or night. Add to that, your horse's head being close to the ground a good deal of the time when eating hay, and clean breathing for him or her in a stall bed on dusty sawdust is highly unlikely. There are also horses that are allergic to the oils in sawdust. Its owner will do well to find sawdust or shavings rendered from kiln dried woods. Otherwise, you'll have a horse with chronic hives and added potential for breathing problems.

Wood Chips. They certainly are pretty. And for the most part, they do their job. They put down a nice bed for the horses to lie on, stand in, and "relieve" themselves. Some wood chips are more absorbent than others. The main problem with wood chips is that they stick to manure, which causes major amounts of waste. Once upon a time, the average barn crew cleaned stalls once a week. Wood chips were great back then. Now stalls are cleaned daily. Cleaning a stall bed on wood chips requires time and discrimination. If cost is an issue, you simply can't go in and start heave-hoeing. You have to be "picky" (no pun intended) in the way you remove the soiled parts of the stall. Otherwise, it's like throwing money out the door. Entertaining the question again about where would a horse lie down out in the wild, we have a retired Thoroughbred broodmare that thinks wood chips are the greatest things on earth. When her stall is bed, she's down and rolling and looks like a wood-chip decorated Christmas tree when she's all said and done. She obviously loves the feel of the soft bedding.

Pine Pellets. These products are great for the backyard barn. You have to start out with a good base, which can be costly. Most manufactures recommend five to six bags to start. But once done, the stalls bed on pine pellets, which plump up when "moisturized" are easy and most efficient. The drawback with the pine pellets, in my opinion, is that they too become dusty. And before very long, look downright dirty, and can get pretty smelly.

The same can be said for Corn Pellets. It's a great way to bed stalls on your own farm, particularly if you only have a few horses. You start with a base, five or six bags, depending on the size of the stall. And you can either lightly wet it down or let your horse's urine wet it down. You only pick out the manure, and leave all but the heaviest wet spots. This is part of the process and it's a breeze cleaning a stall bed this way. The problem I had with the corn pellets was that other people in the barn complained about the smell. It was fine during the summer, when all the doors and windows were open. But once fall hit and the barn was closed up at night, the smell became somewhat overwhelming to some come morning. The most common comment was that it smelled like "sour corn mash."

Whatever the product one chooses, it's important to keep your horse's stall clean and as dust-free as possible, with a solid base for good footing and for when they lie down. I've seen barns where all the bedding is on the walls and very little in the center of the stalls. The logic behind that makes no sense to me. I'm not into stock piling the bedding so I can pull it into the middle two or three days from now. A horse's stall should be bed to work its best day in and day out. Mares need a little extra bedding around the perimeter of their stall. Geldings need extra bedding in the center of their stalls. Some horses are easier to clean up after than others. Some go in one place, some drag whatever they've done everywhere. It should only take a few days of cleaning a horse's stall to determine their patterns. Bed accordingly.

Swine Flu Vaccination

Should We Be Concerned for Our Horses?
Should We Be Concerned for Ourselves?

Fear of a Swine Flu epidemic is enough to make one think of heading for the hills away from civilization, and if you're anything like me, taking your horses with you. There are numerous strains of flu viruses circulating at any given time, year round; viruses that affect humans and animals alike. And while a faraway hill sounds tempting, even if I could saddle up and go, from what I understand it would have to be the perfect hill. Not too cold, or not too dry. It would have to be a Goldilocks just right.

"Flu incidence peaks in the winter season in temperate parts of the world, generally described as areas outside the tropics. Cold and dry conditions help the virus survive outside the body, meaning that droplet particles take longer to evaporate and remain airborne for more extended periods in winter. Influenza outbreaks do occur in the tropics, though less frequently than in areas with less heat and humidity, and without the seasonality seen in areas with wintry weather," according to a study by Asia One.

I would have thought it to be the opposite; the colder the better. But apparently dry cold air is not necessarily a good thing when it comes to viral contagions. The little germies figuratively spread their cold little wings and fly high and low. On the other hand, it's speculated that moist warm climates may actually slow them down.

I vaccinate our horses for influenza. But at the same time, hesitate getting a flu vaccination myself. I'm not sure that kind of logic makes good sense. I initially started vaccinating our horses because it was required at the stables where we boarded. It was a show barn and horses came and went on a regular basis. The decision was not mine. It was part of the cohabitating process. The influenza vaccination I give our horses is not for Swine Flu.

When it comes time to vaccinate our horses, I always ask our trusted veterinarian, "What do you give your horses?" And follow suit. So, why oh why, is it such a difficult decision when it comes to getting a flu vaccination for me personally? I don't want the flu. Who does? I can't imagine anyone saying, Me, Me, I do!

For most of my life, when someone said they had the flu, it meant they were sick. Not that they were dying. And yet, Swine flu has the potential to kill. Should we feel morally obligated to have a Swine Flu vaccine, particularly, when we are out and about, coming and going, much like the horses in a public barn. If I lived on that proverbial hill away from civilization, there would be no question. I would assume I wouldn't need it. No shot for me, thank you. But! I am out and about in the populated world every day. I hug my elderly neighbor. I shake hands with the salesman at my door. I push a grocery cart. Who am I to take a stand and refuse?

Maybe my thinking and anyone else struggling with the decision as to whether or not to get the Swine Flu vaccination, goes back to that rugged individualism our parents and grandparents were so proud of. Maybe we think of the Swine Flu vaccine as a weakness on our part. Maybe we're thinking; I'm tough, I can ward off the flu. I can handle it. But then again, maybe not...maybe we can't handle it. Maybe we're afraid the vaccine itself will make us sick.

Horses: Bullies
They're Not Just on the Playground
They're in the Pasture Too

As a horse lover, I'd like to think there is no such thing as a mean horse. But that simply is not true. I've seen my share and while some had underlying issues such as lameness, illness, or the fact that they were being ill fed that could account for their behavior - some horses appear to be mean without any apparent reason at all. They're mean to their handlers; they're mean to other horses.

I don't like mean horses. I have no use for them. There was one years ago that for some reason took a liking to me, but even then, I had to watch his every move. He'd turn on you in a flash. I'm a gentle handler. I don't relish getting rough with a horse. But I don't like getting bit, kicked, or stepped on either. A person has to always be on guard when dealing with a horse with aggressive habits. You need to be firm. Not mean, firm. You can't fight with a horse, particularly a horse that likes fighting back.

If you raised the horse and know its history and know it has never been mishandled, then its meanness might very well be genetics. I'm of the opinion that personality runs in families. Kind gentle horses, as a rule, pass on those kind gentle traits. Aggressive behavior runs in families, too. A bully on the other hand is not necessarily mean. And odds are he or she does have issues that can be addressed. Does he need more work? Does she need less work? Is he used to being fed first? Does she have to be the first horse out in the pasture and the first one in? Why? Does she or he need a full door on the stall? Does a full door make them paranoid? Does being able to look out make them happier, less aggressive? Sometimes the opposite of standard thinking is the key.

Is she or he getting too much grain? Too little? Are they standing too many hours in their stall? Do they eat all their hay too quickly? This could be an indication of a horse that has gone without to an extreme somewhere in his past; a horse that may have had to fight for every blade of grass or flake of hay. Horses are a little like elephants. They never forget.

A horse unsure of his next meal has reason to be mean. They don't like being hungry. Who does? Horses with this history do best to have free choice hay and no grain. Sometimes that's all it takes to settle them down and make them useful. A horse that is being fed too much is just as serious a problem. They have too much energy, and if the work level is not such that all that energy is being expended, then you're going to see that energy in the form of aggression and crankiness, or just plain "feeling their oats" with other horses and you to an extreme.

A bully should be made to pay for his behavior, but not necessarily how one might think. Horses are herd animals, and in my horse world, I am herd leader. I will not tolerate a horse bullying other horses. If he or she doesn't straighten up and stop picking on the other horses, then he or she gets turned out alone, and all the better if it is full sight of the other horses so they know what they're missing. A week or two and most can be turned out with the herd again, and properly behave. Horses will play, horses will spar. It's part of establishing dominance. Meanness, per se, has no part in this. It might appear so, but watch closely. When does the sparring stop? And if one horse walks or runs away, does the other one still want to fight. If that's the case, then that's a bully. They don't belong on the playground with the other kids, and they don't belong in a pasture with other horses. Being a bully is stressful. Remove the horse from that trumped up role, and odds are you will have a happier horse to be around yourself. He or she may thank you.

Severe Weather Warning - Tornado Season Safety for You and Your Horse

In the novel "Hannah's Home," Hannah weathers a tornado in the barn with her horse Billy Bob. She survives, her horse survives. It's fiction. Riding out a storm in the barn is not exactly recommended. For years, people have been told in cases of severe weather such as tornadoes and hurricanes that an animal is safer outside. They have natural instincts of survival that we humans don't. I have observed some of our horses over the years showing great instincts. They turn their back to the wind; they put a foal in the center of the herd. They hunker down and ride out the storm, apparently as nature intended, stoic and with resignation.

The same horse that literally goes bonkers when someone is walking overhead in the hayloft will stand in thunder and lightning as if it is an everyday occurrence. Some horses though, are afraid of storms. They don't like the sounds of them; they don't like the looks of them. They don't want any part of them. At the first rumble of distant thunder or gust of wind whipping up, they're at the barn door or gate wanting inside, now! I have one horse that will whinny at the barn door as if sounding an alarm for the entire world to hear.

In lightning and thunder, a horse is safer inside the barn. All barns should have lightning rods on their roofs. Do you go running out in a lightning storm to bring the horses in from distant pastures, no. If they are near the barn and you still have time before the storm hits, yes, by all means, bring them inside. Give them some extra hay, shut the barn doors, and go back to the house. If weather prevents you a safe retreat inside your home, or you are at the boarding stable, don't panic. Head for an area that has no windows, be it the feed room, the tack room, the bathrooms. And stay there, until the sounds of the storm have passed.

Little Angel

It was a warm star-lit May night in Northeast Ohio. Officially still spring, it felt more like summer. All the barn chores were done and we'd decided to go to a Drive-In movie with my husband's brother Jeff and his wife Linda. We don't go out much and neither do they. We're either too busy, or too tired. I'm not complaining, mind you. We love farm life. Not one of us would trade it for anything else, though every once in a while, it is nice to get away for a few hours.

Pixie Dust, the chestnut Quarter Horse I'd shown as a teenager was due to foal, but that wasn't for another week or so. Tonight was the best night for us to go. Tomorrow we'd be haying. We all piled into the dually, brought our own popcorn and soft drinks, some chocolate fudge made from our own goat's milk, and headed into town.

The movie was supposed to be a comedy, but right off I didn't like it and wasn't laughing. The longer it went on, the more agitated I became. Linda and I ate all the fudge, one piece after another, and playfully fought over the crumbs; the only funny highlight of the evening thus far. When our husbands had heard enough of our complaining, mine suggested we go back to the house and watch our "Field of Dreams" video. How many times would that be, a hundred maybe? Off we went.

As we pulled down the driveway I got a strange feeling, one of those nagging "women things" as John calls them. "I'm going to go check on Pixie," I said. They all followed. I love sneaking into the barn this time of night. It's so calm and peaceful. Sometimes just before going to bed I put on my housecoat and go out and just marvel as I gaze around at the horses and cows. They hardly stir; their eyes half asleep amidst a hushed symphony of sound. The dogs all smile at me and wag their tails from deep inside their straw beds.

Pixie is fine, standing at the back of her stall resting one hind leg. When we quietly turn to leave, I see her shift her weight to the other hind leg. I hesitate and wait for her usual contented sigh. As I lean against the stall door I notice a path in her stall, not deep, not too obvious, but I know my mare. She's been pacing. I look at my husband, and he knows that something is not right.

I suggest they go on inside, that I'll straighten up Pixie's stall and join them in a minute. I tell them where the movie is and motion again for them to go. But they all just stand there. Pixie lost her last foal. John and I came out in the morning that day to find it dead, lying in the back of the stall, and still completely in its sack. I think a part of me died that day, too. It was a perfect little filly, chestnut like Pixie, a little white strip on its gentle little face. I stand like a statue, reliving that moment, and feel a hand on my shoulder.

"I'll get it," my husband says, meaning he'll straighten up the stall. I step back out of the way, wiping tears from my eyes.

"Um, how 'bout I bring the portable TV out here," Jeff suggests, and we all try to laugh. What happened last year was a fluke, from all accounts. For some reason, the sack didn't open during birth. It usually does. No sooner had John cleaned and straightened Pixie's stall, she started pacing again. Within five minutes, her water broke.

"It's show time," John said, another manly attempt to lighten the mood as he rolled up his sleeves. How many calves had he helped come into this world, how many lambs? How many foals? But this is Pixie Dust. This is my mare. When she goes down, I hover at her side, stroking her neck. She's sweat from head to toe, straining, her eyes glazing over.

"Oh, God, what if she dies," I think. "What if…?"

"The foal's coming," I hear John say, but I can't look. All I can see is the pain in Pixie's eyes, her nostrils flaring with each labored breath. "Don't die, Pixie," I whisper. Why do I think she's going to die? "Don't die…."

I hear a swooshing sound. Out of the corner of my eye I can see my brother-in-law bend down slowly onto one knee. His expression frightens me. Another dead foal, I just know it. I see his shoulders slump. I look at my sister-in-law, our eyes lock on one another's. Then she turns back. She's holding her breath; I can tell she's afraid to breathe. She clutches her hands to her chest, leaning in further and further. Then I see her smile. She looks at me and nods.

"It's okay! It's okay," she says, and I dare take a look. John is holding the foal in his arms, blood and mess all over him and the foal looking dazed, but very much alive. "It's okay!"

I turn back to Pixie, hug her, tell her the good news, but she's not moving. She's just lying there, taking each heavy breath as if it is her last. I hug her again. I tell her I love her. I tell her that over and over and over as she looks up at me, her eyes searching mine. I feel her slipping away, getting weaker and weaker. She nickers, a tiny soft little nicker, for me, for her foal…. I bite hard at my bottom lip, stroke her mane, and turn to see my husband, on his knees, carrying the foal to Pixie's side.

"Come on, girl," he says, with big tears running down his face. "Say hi to your little one. Come on." He places the foal in my lap, and Pixie lifts her head to nuzzle it. She licks its face, and then its neck, and nickers again. She wants the baby closer to her, and then even closer. She looks at all of us anxiously, as if we are in the way, and nuzzles her babe again and again, gaining more and more strength with each touch of her newborn.

"Let's try and get her up," John says. Pixie attempts to rise several times, but is so weak. We all pray, first silently and then out loud. When she finally stands, we all cry. Our attention immediately goes to the foal then. We need to get it onto its feet, get it to nurse. It wobbles and teeters. Pixie licks it again and again, nudging it to her side, and finally we succeed in getting it to suckle.

When both the mare and the foal were all taken care of, my husband cleaned up the afterbirth and put some more straw down in the stall. The foal lay back down and Pixie sighed contentedly, then took a drink of water and started munching on some hay. By the time my sister-in-law left and came back with a pot of coffee, a feeling of quiet calm had returned to the barn.

"I've never seen a mare act like that in labor," John said. "I thought we'd lost her."

"Me too," I said softly, shuddering at the thought.

"I'm glad we left the movie," Jeff said, and we all agreed.

The following morning, as I stood gazing at Pixie Dust and her absolutely perfect little chestnut filly with a tiny white star on its forehead, I couldn't have been happier. This would be Pixie's only foal. In the wee hours of the night, we decided to never breed her again. Her labors were obviously too hard on her and this foal, too, had been born completely in the sack. John had to tear it open. If we hadn't been there with her, this foal probably would have died as well. Pixie had no strength to help.

How close had she been to dying, to leaving this precious little foal behind? Thankfully, we will never know. We are convinced as she was slipping away, her foal called her back. We've named this newborn filly, "Little Angel," because that's what she is. She's our "Little Angel." And we couldn't love her more.

For the Love of Horses

From the time I was a little child of but five-years old, I have loved horses. I loved them because they were beautiful. I loved them because they were kind. I loved them because they ran fast. I loved them because smelled good. I loved sitting on their backs and shaking the reins. I loved saying "giddy up."

Most children outgrow horses. It would be hard telling when looking at a group of budding equestrians, who will still be riding as adults. Something clicks, and for that person, that one in a hundred, there can never possibly be a life without horses.

Our daughter lost interest in horses after riding as a child. Then for some reason, seemingly out of the blue, she bought a horse of her own as an adult. She was back in the game. "I fell in love," she says jokingly, but is serious. It's hard to say what clicks with a particular horse and owner. It just happens. She looked at Johnny C and that was that. She had to have him.

"I can't imagine a life without horses," Cindy T. says. "I bought my first racehorse in my twenties and I've been hooked ever since. I grew up with horses. My sister owned and showed Thoroughbreds. I actually don't recall ever not being around horses."

Horse owners dish out hundreds of dollars each month, and this for an animal they "visit" elsewhere and see perhaps an hour a day. Most often they are paying a trainer or instructor to help them become an even better owner and rider. They might not be with that horse every moment of the day, but for the most part, they're thinking about them. They're thinking about that next visit, that next ride, that next show. They're thinking about taking their friends to visit, their families.

Horse owners do without something personally, so that their horse can have it all. Imagine making an appointment with a "shoe person" every eight weeks to have your "shoes" done. Imagine routinely getting "new shoes" without feeling guilty, because, hey, your shoe person says you need them.

Imagine getting a brand new winter blanket (I mean, uh winter parka) every year, because, be honest, you abused the last one. You chewed on it, you kicked at it. You lay down and rolled in the mud and muck in it, over and over, and over.

Imagine a life where someone doesn't spray you to keep the flies away. Imagine not having a new saddle pad at least twice a year, and preferably with your name embroidered on it. Imagine not going to a horse show to strut your stuff. Imagine a life without your human. Imagine a life without your horse. Do you love horses?

Love is a relationship. It's caring. It's nurturing. It's all consuming. It's long hours in the barn. It's a schooling session again and again. It's a trail ride in the park. It's a walk. It's a path.

Christmas Eve

David always hung the Christmas tree lights in the Johnson household. It was a family tradition. The children were anxious, Julie was anxious. He'd gone into town to pick up milk and was late. In all the scurrying around getting ready for Christmas Eve dinner, Julie had forgotten it. There wouldn't be a store open anywhere in Larksbury tomorrow, not even the gas station.

Julie stared out the window. With six inches of fresh snow on the ground and more expected overnight, she worried. Their old pickup was on its last legs. It needed transmission fluid practically every day now, and the four-wheel drive no longer worked. Their farm was located exactly ten miles from the heart of town. David should have been home an hour ago.

She took out the coloring books and started coloring with the children. Becky was three; Jeremy was five; two darling little freckled-faced red-headed kids. When Julie finally spotted the headlights of their truck coming up the drive, she did a double take. There was another set of headlights on its heels. Her parents used to come for Christmas Eve dinner, but they were both gone now. For a moment, she forgot that. She strained to see through the falling snow. It was another pickup truck, pulling a horse trailer. David motioned for the driver to park up close to the barn. Julie wiped the window pane with her sleeve, trying to recognize the young man when he got out of the truck, and then the young woman.

Jeremy piled onto the couch next to her. "Who's that?"

"I don't know," Julie said, wrapping her arm around him.

David and the young couple trudged through the snow to the back of the horse trailer, the snow pelting their faces as they opened it and lowered the ramp. The young man disappeared inside.

Becky climbed up next to Jeremy. "It's a pony! It's a pony!"

Julie chuckled. Both children already had ponies. Besides this was a horse, a very large horse, heavily blanketed. David opened the barn doors and led the way inside. Julie glanced at Becky and Jeremy, and was debating whether to bundle them up and go out to investigate, when they heard a soft knock on the door. Jeremy got to it first, and flung it open. There stood the young woman, shivering. Julie ushered her in. "Are you all right?"

"The truck has no heat," the little waif said, teeth chattering. "The windows were frosting over. I kept trying to talk to keep it from freezing, my breath you know, but...."

Julie guided her to the hearth of the fireplace, where a rip-roaring fire crackled. "Here, sit down. I'll get you some tea."

The children crumpled onto the floor next to the woman. "Are you make believe?" Becky asked.

The woman smiled. "No, I'm for real. My n-n-n-name is Marie." She looked at Julie. "I'm sorry, this being Christmas Eve and all. I don't know what we would have done if your husband hadn't offered us shelter."

Shelter? Julie stared. Were they planning to stay the night? Where would she put them? The young woman must have read her thoughts. "I'm fine right here. John, my husband, will be too. We won't be any bother, I promise you. It's Maggie Mae we're concerned about. She's due to foal."

"When?" Julie asked. Surely not tonight.

"Not for a couple of weeks, but...." She gripped the mug of tea in her gloved hands and took a sip. "Thank you. We're not poor or anything, not really. We just don't have any money."

Julie laughed. "I know the feeling."

David and the young woman's husband came inside and dusted themselves off.

"Daddy!!"

"The milk," David said, handing the gallon jug to Julie and hugging the kids. "Do you know where that old heat lamp is?"

"Why?" Julie asked. "Is she...?"

"We're not sure. She acts like she might be."

"Ma'am," John said, tipping his head.

"Hello," Julie replied, reverting her attention quickly back to David. "It's in the garage, over by the rakes. I don't think the bulb still works though."

David headed back outside with John right behind him. Julie busied herself with setting the table. She'd made chili for dinner, and as usual, made a big batch for freezing some. There would be plenty. Becky and Jeremy entertained the young woman, who by now was warming up and peeling off her gloves, then her scarf and coat, and then one of two sweaters she was wearing.

When the men returned - yes, they were in luck, the lamp worked. Julie gave them each a mug of strong coffee and when they'd warmed enough, motioned for everyone to sit down and eat. It was going to be a long night. The mare was waxing up and restless; warm now, but restless. Julie looked across the table at her husband, the kindest man she'd ever known. Their eyes met for a second and he smiled.

"So, where ya'll going, and where are you from?" David asked, after he'd said grace and they'd all started eating. These details weren't all that significant when he'd encountered them in town - John beside himself with worry trying to find a place to stay and Marie in tears.

"Hendersonville."

"I know the place," David said, passing the cornbread and then the pitcher of milk. "I've been there. It's a right nice town."

John and Marie squeezed one another's hands. "We're hoping so."

Outside it began to snow even harder, big white flakes that swirled and whirled in the howling wind. David said he'd check out their truck in the morning and see if he could fix it. "I've got truck parts everywhere," he added, laughing when Julie nodded in agreement.

"I think you'll be comfortable in the kid's room," Julie said. "The kids can sleep with us."

"Yeah!!! Yippee!!" Jeremy and Becky shouted! "Yippee!"

"Well, we wouldn't want to disappoint the children," Marie said, accepting the offer with tears welling up in her eyes. Both couples had lifetimes to share. Conversation flowed easy. When the meal was finished, Marie helped Julie clean up, and David and John went back out to the barn to check on the mare. David returned a few minutes later.

"Ya'll might want to come out," he said. "The kids too. She's got her a healthy foal. It's a little colt." They all bundled up, filled with anticipation and trudged out into the snow.

Soon they were all gathered around the mare's stall and watched as the tiny babe nursed hungrily, tail swishing.

"I don't even want to think about what would have happened if we hadn't found shelter." John's voice cracked. "She'd have been in that trailer, and...."

"Shhhh," Julie said. "Everything is fine. Look how beautiful he is."

John put his arm around his wife Marie, as above the barn, a star shined bright.

"Thank you."

Indigo Horses - Myth, Mystery, Magic

As a child, I always dreamed of owning a gray horse. The grays were my favorites at the racetrack. They were my favorites at the riding stable. They were my favorites everywhere. I don't know if it was because there were fewer gray horses than others, or one in particular. I don't recall every actually riding a gray horse, growing up. But they were there, though few and far between, and I coveted them.

I bought my first horse at age eighteen and went looking for a gray but ended up with a bay roan. On a bright summer day, he almost had the look of a gray horse, but for his brown face and black legs, mane, forelock and tail. The trademark dark flecks of solid color on the bodies of roans are called corn marks. He had them all over.

There are strawberry roans, which is a mixture of reddish colored hair with white hair. Their manes, forelocks and tails are mostly red with some white hairs intermingled. A blue roan had black body hair mixed with white and has a black tail, mane, legs and forelock. A bay roan is just as it sounds. Bay colored hair and white are mixed, with the same "black points" as a blue roan.

When a roan sheds out in the summer they will appear lighter, but this is the case with most horses. The roans' darker hair will always be their true color. Their dark hair does not turn white. In contrast, a gray horse's hair will lighten with age, but they will always be gray, even when they look totally white, because of their gray mane and tail. A true white horse has a white mane and tail.

But what about the color of the Indigo Horse, the true Indigo Horse, and does an Indigo Horse truly exist?

Are these horses dark gray or are they a blue roan? Are they blue-black? Can a solid black horse be an Indigo Horse? Is an Indigo Horse one that shimmers the color blue in the sunlight? Do their backs reflect the light of the blue moon? Do Indigo Horses have a blue aura? Do they have blue eyes?

A definition of the color indigo, according to Merriam-Webster's Online Dictionary is a (blue vat dye obtained from plants as in indigo plants) the principal coloring matter $C_{16}H_{10}N_2O_2$ of natural indigo usually synthesized as a blue powder with a coppery luster, a deep reddish blue.

Deep reddish blue? A Coppery luster? This definition sounds more like it would be the color of a chestnut horse, a deep liver chestnut horse perhaps. I have seen dogs that possess all of these colors, but a horse? A mystical Indigo Horse?

The Encyclopedia Britannica states Indigo is: in botany, any shrub or herb of the genus Indigofera within the pea family. Most species occur in warm climates and are generally silky or hairy. The leaves are usually divided into smaller leaflets. The small rose, purple, or white flowers are borne in spikes or clusters.

Rose colored flowers, purple flowers, white flowers? Sounds like a blue roan or a strawberry roan, perhaps, but definitely a horse of different colors, a horse whose coat is silky and deep reddish blue. The Indigo Horse, myth, mystery…magic. Pegasus can fly.

"The Indigo Horse knows."

From the Boarding Stable to Your Back Yard
Bringing Your Horse Home

Any number of circumstances can lead up to the decision to bring your horse home. It could be that you no longer ride, or that your horse can no longer be ridden. Maybe it's a combination of both. Maybe it's for financial reasons. Maybe it's simply that you want your horse home and that you want to be in charge of his or her care.

If you have the property and you are "zoned" for horses, this is a dream come true for many. You have an existing barn, or perhaps you have just built a barn. You have a paddock and/or pasture. You have the knowledge, or you're learning. You have the desire.

There are pros and cons for having your horse at home. People tend to ride more when their horse is stabled at a boarding facility. Maybe it's to justify the money spent to board the horse, particularly in these economic times. Maybe it's because of the fact that you have other boarders to ride with. It's a very special social time for you. It's as if you belong to a horse style country club. Everyone gets to know one another. They look out for one another. It's fun! Having an indoor arena to ride all year long is an added bonus.

By the same token, your horse is your best "horse" friend. And you'll want to consider what's best for him and her, as well as yourself. Will your horse be happy at home? Will he or she adjust to being alone? We had a retired thoroughbred that lived on our farm for three years by himself. He was as happy as can be alone. He got all the attention he'd shared with his barn mates/pasture mates for years.

On the other hand, I have a Morgan mare that

would go bonkers on her own. I would not be doing her justice, or any horse like her, having them in a backyard alone. They would miss the herd-like socialization and perhaps so will you.

You'll have to do your research. Know what your horse's feed costs and where to buy it, decide what type of bedding you're going to use. Know how you are going to dispose of your horse's manure, or what it takes to turn it into good fertilizer. You don't want to be sprouting oats in your vegetable garden with "too fresh" manure. You don't want the neighbor complaining you are contaminating their well water with your big manure pile either.

Find a good hay source, one you can rely on. Make sure you have secure fencing. Make sure if you need a pasture mate for your horse that the horse comes on a trial. Horses have likes and dislikes, and if they don't get along, there's going to be trouble.

Thus said, I can tell you from first-hand experience, there's nothing like that first cup of coffee, looking out your kitchen window at your horses grazing lazily in the morning sun. Plan ahead, do your homework, cover all your basis, and should you decide...bring your horse home.

Winter Water Buckets

It goes without saying that water is the single most important nutrient in your horse's life. I know have stressed this before, but with cold temperatures upon us, it bears repeating. Extreme heat of summer calls for extra diligence and so does the dead of winter. Horses need an ample amount of "drinkable" water at all times. A half-frozen water bucket doesn't cut it. If you know your horses' water buckets are going to freeze overnight, then you need to do something about it. Imagine your efforts to be "life-saving" to your horse, because they are.

At a lot of barns, as soon as the temperature drops, hoses are disconnected to keep them from freezing. During the day and if it warms up, they can be reconnected and used, but for the most part, inevitably the watering is eventually done by the bucket load and takes extra commitment. Do not put cold water on top of a half frozen bucket of water, thinking it will thaw the rest. Yes, the temperature is higher than freezing, and in a perfect case scenario, in time it would thaw that block of ice, similar to thawing a frozen turkey in cold water. But, your horse is going to drink that fresh water, and very soon, that bucket will be back to being half frozen and maybe even thicker.

Bucket warmers can be used to keep the water above freezing. There are various designs of bucket warmers that come as one piece, some as adaptations for current water buckets. They work. And they are not expensive when you spread the cost out over a period of three months. A heated water bucket can be purchased for approximately $35. That's about thirty-nine cents a day. Yes, it will take electricity, and that has to be figured into the cost. But with the average price of a veterinarian farm call for a horse that is impacted and colicky, again, it is worth the investment.

There are also heating elements that can be purchased at the tack stores for warming water. Use them according to directions. If, whether it is a financial issue or "electrical" safety issue and bucket warmers and heating elements cannot be used - perhaps your boarding stable won't allow them - they aren't wired for them - they just don't want them. Then insist that the buckets be dumped daily and filled with fresh water.

If hot water is available, whether at the pump area of the barns or the bathrooms, fill a container to top off the water buckets with the hot water. If hot water is not available in the barn, then bring hot water in plastic gallon jugs from home and top off the water in the buckets. One bucket or two, treat them both the same. Your horse will thank you, over and over. A healthy horse is a happy horse.

Thoroughbred at the Track

Day Seven Before the Race

This article begins a seven-part series documenting a week in the life of a Thoroughbred racehorse. The horse is a four-year old gelding. He had been in training for two months this season before his first start and has run three times. He finished sixth; came back tired, a third; came back a little muscle sore, and ran a fourth. His last race when he placed fourth was three days ago. The condition of that race was non-winners for the year, claiming price $20,000 down to $17,500, three-year-olds and up. He was beaten only a length and a half. As the saying goes, "He ran big but came up short."

There is a great deal of importance placed on past performances in a racehorse. But for the most part, that horse and his career exist in the now. When a racehorse wins a race, he *"win"* the race, present tense. Even if he won the race two years ago, it's still a win. This particular horse is looking for his first win this year. Past, future, present, it's all about the moment.

It'll be his first day back to the track after his last race. He ran six furlongs, came back good, and as is customary, was given two days off. He was hand-walked the first day, and was hung on the walking machine the second day. Hung, odd term, but that's how it's said. The expression simply means he's hooked up to the machine and is walked mechanically. A horse that is hand-walked usually gets about fifteen to twenty turns around the shedrow. A shedrow is the working area of the barn, a path under the eave where one walks and cools out the horses. An average barn has about twenty-five stalls on each side, so it's a good long walk. A horse hung on the walking machine will walk for about half an hour.

Day Six Before the Race

Charting a horse for a race can be complicated. Luckily, the best day for this horse to run has two conditions to choose from. That is not usually the case. There is a $15,000 claiming race going six furlongs, non-winners this year, and a $17,500 claiming race, non-winners this year, going seven-eighths of a mile. The ideal distance for this horse, particularly the way he ran last time out, is six furlongs. He'll be lot a stronger at the end. But, it would be running him for a claiming price that is less than what he is worth. There is always the possibility he could be claimed.

The trainer has the exercise person gallop the horse two miles today. The horse comes back dancing and prancing. It's a cool morning, the track is fast. The two-mile gallop didn't take much out of him. When he's hung on the walking machine, he starts bucking. The trainer watches him for a moment and is just about to have the groom take the horse off and hand-walk him, when the horse settles down.

The blacksmith comes by to check out that one hind shoe that always gives the horse trouble. It spread a little this morning in training and has to be reset. The blacksmith is careful not to trim the hoof. He is as non-invasive as possible. The concern would be, even if the horse came up a little tender, they wouldn't enter him.

The horse's owner shows up at the barn and the trainer tactfully discourages him from giving the horse too many carrots. The trainer treats the man to breakfast at the track kitchen and they go over their race choices. This particular trainer is not above discussing the condition book with the owner, but insists on having the final say. This owner is "good pay;" the ideal owner in that aspect. His training bills, vet bills, and blacksmith bills are always paid on time. The man can be a little opinionated, but not overbearing. He listens to reason. Owner and trainer is a unique partnership.

Day Five Before the Race

The racehorse was to be given a day off today, but is too wound up. He's kicking the stall wall and squealing and wheeling in his stall. If he spreads that hind shoe again, there will be no racing him this week. The trainer decides to have the horse ponied; no-rider, just cantered alongside a lead pony. The pony, a tough rock-solid Appaloosa, who's seen it all and done it all and the pony rider will have their "hands   full."

The Thoroughbred is done up in felt bandages on all four legs before he goes to the track to protect him from injury. This is precisely why the pony is always done up in all fours, too. He needs protection as well. Pony horses are priceless. The really good ones are as dear as a racehorse. The racehorse starts out bucking and kicking, but settles down nicely after about a quarter of a mile. He canters alongside the pony in stride. When he gets back to the barn he is given a bath and is hand-walked, as the walking machine is full.

There's a loose horse running between barns. This stirs all the horses, including this one being hand-walked.

His groom puts him in the stall to try to settle him down, but he's gotten himself all wound up again and has broken out in a sweat. Fortunately the loose horse is caught quickly, and the groom gets his horse back out and talks him into quieting down as he walks him round and around the shedrow. Several horses charge their stall guards as they pass, but soon they too settle back down.

When the horse is put back in his stall, he's given a good rubdown and is done up. He stands munching his hay and playfully kicks out at his groom. He's scolded, and seems to smile at the groom's reprimand in reaction to his antics. This groom is superstitious. When he leaves the stall, he looks back twice. Tomorrow he will look back three times. The trainer shakes his head.

Day Four Before the Race

It rained all night. There's a thunderstorm still going on. It's a wasted day. The racetrack is closed for training because of the lightning. The horses can't be put on the walker machines because of the lightning. All the horses in the barns are wound up, kicking their stalls and bucking and playing. The shedrow is too wet and too slippery to even safely hand-walk the horses. The hope is that the thunderstorms will let up to allow racing this afternoon. If so, the horses not running today can at least be put on the walking machines then.

The track kitchen is packed with trainers and exercise boys and girls (yes, they are still called boys and girls, even though most of them are men and women). The cooks can't fry up eggs fast enough. Talk is loud to try and drown out the heavy rain on the kitchen's tin roof. There is laughter. While this could possibly be considered a nice break from normal routine, there isn't a horseperson there, who wouldn't rather be training. The door opens and yet another trainer - clad in a yellow slicker, enters and shakes off the rain, muttering an obscenity.

Day Three Before the Race

There's a power outage at the racetrack this morning. More than one horseman jokes that it's probably because the guys at the clubhouse (the track managers) haven't paid the bill. The electricity comes back on a little after 9:00 a.m. Training had continued throughout. There was plenty of daylight, but for about an hour, there was no water for water buckets or bathing, or for the rest rooms in the barn area.

Whether or not a race will fill is always a gamble and, similar to handicapping one plays the odds. Some conditions fill routinely, particularly conditions for non-winners. Some conditions - it's harder to field enough horses for the race to go. The trainer decides their best chance is the race going seven-eighths of a mile for $17,500 non-winners this year. He stares at the training chart. With that in mind and the fact that the horse has been "higher than a kite" he instructs the exercise person to "two-minute lick" the horse. It's a racetrack expression that simply means he wants the horse to be galloped the mile at a two-minute pace.

As a comparison, a good time for a horse running a mile race is a minute and thirty eight seconds. A two minute lick is a good pace for a gallop and the horse should come back strong. The horse is backed up first at a trot.

When the exercise person turns him around and clicks to him, the horse is feeling good and bucks several times.

When he settles down, it's all business. He gallops like a stake horse and comes back tossing his head and snorting. During his bath, he paws and chews the end of his lead shank. From all indications, he feels great and will be as ready as he'll ever be for the race.

When the groom does his legs up, he notices a small cut on the inside of his left hock. Instinctively he checks that troublesome hind shoe. It's still intact. He dabs some ointment on the cut, and upon leaving the stall, looks back three times. The horse charges the webbing playfully and chases him out. The groom laughs.

Day Two Before the Race

If the horse was going to run three quarters of a mile in two days, this would be the morning he'd be breezed a half mile. Breezing is not as strenuous as a work, but it would tighten him up and get him ready. Since the trainer has decided to run him in the condition that is seven-eighths of a mile, today he will be galloped two miles instead.

The horse is feeling good! It's a cool crisp morning and he is eager to run. He tries to run off for about a quarter of a mile, but settles nicely going into the first turn. He gallops strong and comes back dancing and prancing and kicks out at a horse in passing. The horse kicks back; they are nowhere near in range to connect, and both exercise riders laugh.

The track is closed immediately after they exit at the gap as there has been an accident up by the quarter pole. Both exercise riders turn to look. There's nothing funny anymore. The injured horse is hobbling, enough so to see even from this distance. And its jock is limping alongside the horse. The track ambulance staff goes into action.

The horse due to run in two days gets back to the barn and is given a bath. He is hung on the walking machine to cool out and then is put into his stall and done up. When the trainer entered the horse early this morning, there were four other horses already entered for the race. The other condition only had two entries. Where he'd entered seemed like a sure bet. But the seven-eighths race did not go. A few minutes before entries closed, the trainer was paged to the secretary's office. Having the horse go from being targeted to run seven-eighths of a mile for $17,500 to three quarters of a mile for $15,000 is big. That shorter distance makes all the difference in the world, even with the drop in price. For those that might not think so, they should stop and think of how many races are lost or won in the last five to ten strides to the wire.

Day One Before the Race

Today is a day of waiting. The horse is hand-walked this morning and on-the-muscle. He's in the seventh race tomorrow and has drawn the number five position in an eleven horse field. The trainer has nine other horses in the barn in various stages of their training. Three are galloped, two ponied. One is running today, and the others are walked. Mid-morning, feed and hay is delivered, and the blacksmith comes by to shoe one of the horses. He checks the horses entered for today and tomorrow and says they're good to go.

The horse's owner arrives at the barn. He's completely supportive of the trainer's decision, but is worried. He asks again, "Are you sure that's the best place to run him?"

The trainer says, "Yes," and explains, "He's not making you any money standing in the barn. If anybody takes him, they're going to run into the same problem as us. No races. If he wins and they take him, we'll buy something better. Remember what I told you when you got into this business, you don't fall in love with the horses."

The horse's groom frowns. "I do. They better *not* take him." He is cutting out a patch ahead of time to cover the small cut on the horse's hind leg in the race tomorrow. If the horse wins, the groom will receive what is referred to as a "stake." It's a tip of sorts, a little something extra for taking such good care of the horse. Depending on the amount of the purse, the stake can be anywhere from ten dollars to a hundred dollars or even more. This particular owner is very generous with stakes, the trainer too. If the horse wins and gets claimed, the groom will still get a stake from them both, but he will also get a broken heart.

Race Day

On just about any day of the week there is a horse in the barn scheduled to run. It's routine, and played out all over the backside of the racetrack, but never taken for granted. The horse is given his usual scoop of oats for breakfast. He is hand-walked around the shedrow and is put back into his stall as soon as his stall is cleaned. He will not get any hay today until after the race. This is to insure he does not run on a full belly, which would not be healthy or efficient, as with any athlete.

The horse will not have anything done with him until just before the race. When that time comes, he will be groomed and done up in running bandages and the patch will be applied over the cut on the inside of his hind leg. He will have his mouth rinsed just before his groom puts his bridle on him, then starts the walk to the paddock.

The trainer looks at the racing form for at least the tenth time that day, and then glances at the tote board. His horse's odds of 7-2 haven't changed since this morning. He's still second choice. That's good, he reminds his owner, standing nervously at his side. The horse picked to win the race has been running for $12,500 and has jumped up in price. If the handicappers think this horse can outrun theirs, it makes their horse look less appealing to claim.

The horse enters the paddock looking calm but ready, eager. As he is tacked, his muscles quiver. He tosses his head and chews on the lead shank. His groom talks to him to try to keep him calm. The jockey comes out of the jock's room and the trainer and he talk strategy. Out of the corner of his eye the trainer sees two well-known fellow trainers "clocking" his horse. They are attempting to not look obvious, but no one is fooling anyone. They are trying to figure out if running our horse at the drop in price is for a reason other than the fact that the other race didn't go, which is common knowledge. Has the horse trained poorly this past week? Did he come back sore after his last race? Are they "wanting" him claimed?

The horse is oblivious to any of this. He feels great! He wants to run. "Go to the front and take him with you," the trainer says to his rider. The jockey chuckles. Normally they bring this horse off the pace. "That won't work today," the trainer tells him. "There's not enough speed in the race. You'll make an easy lead."

Right as he says this, the groom takes a not-so-discreet look at the patch on the horse's inside back leg. The glance is maybe a little too obvious. On purpose? Or not? He pats the horse on the neck. "Win!" he whispers.

As a rule, this horse is easy to load in the starting gate. He gives the handlers a little trouble today. When he finally loads, he fidgets. His jock takes hold, goggles in place. The horse's odds have dropped to 3-1. He's still second choice. The favorite is now 5-2. "And they're off!"

Our horse breaks good and by the time they come out of the chute, he's on the lead. He settles nicely down the backside. With two lengths on the favorite, his rider sits and waits for a challenger as they near the 3/8's pole. Around the turn, running the half in 46 seconds flat, he asks for a little run and is impressed with his horse's eagerness to stretch out his lead. As they near the 1/8th pole the rider looks back and sees that they will not be challenged today. Our horse wins in hand by four lengths.

There is a celebration among the trainer and the horse's owner and friends. The horse comes back good. His groom is happy but nervous. There has been a claim in the race. He leads our horse into the Winner's Circle, and then heaves a huge sigh of relief to see that it is not his horse that is claimed, but the horse that ran third.

The win picture is snapped, and the groom struts his horse to the test barn. He looks at the patch on the horse's leg. It has stayed in place, no nicks. Where will they run next? The trainer says not to worry, there is a starter allowance race back in ten days going seven-eighths for $12,500. They'll target him for that, and there will be no risk of claiming. The groom gives his horse a pat and walks alongside proudly. "I knew he'd run big!" The trainer smiles.

Toothache, Sore Back, or Just Plain Misbehavin'? What Seems to Be the Problem?

You're tacking up to ride and notice your horse is a little cranky. She's either pinned her ears as you place the saddle on her back, or he's tried taking a nip out of you as you duck under the crosstie to reach for his bridle. He's picked up a hind leg and poses a threat of a kick when you tighten the girth. She starts pawing in the crossties and never has before. He or she becomes fidgety. What is this all about?

Is it close to dinner time, turnout time? Have you interrupted his or her schedule? Is there another horse nearby aggravating him? "You looking at me?" Is it about to rain? Is there distant thunder rumbling? Is she in heat, or, in regards to a male horse, is there a mare nearby in heat? Is it just plain too hot or too cold? Is there any reason anywhere in the general vicinity that could be the cause for his or her mood?

If not and this is just about you and the horse and the upcoming ride, with behavior that appears to have come on suddenly and from out of nowhere, then you need to take notice. Your horse is trying to tell you something.

A horse moves forward with a pull and push motion, so it makes sense to start at the front. Check for sore spots on the horse's gums and on the roof of his or her mouth. Check for inflamed areas around the teeth. If all seems well with the mouth, move on to the saddle and girth area. Check for "the proverbial burr under the saddle," which in this case could be a cut, a bug bite, a sore back. Run your thumb and index finger down the horse's back.

He or she may be ticklish, so don't press too light. Do not press too hard. Watch for his or her reaction. Do they scrunch down, lower their back? Do they tuck their hindquarters underneath them? Do they just stand there? Any sign of discomfort in the spine and back area will usually show itself with the horse's reaction. Tenderness in the back might be a temporary issue. Or a sign of a more serious nature, a chronic issue that you will want to address with your veterinarian.

If you observe the way a horse reacts negatively to being tacked, it becomes apparent that he or she associates the entire process to his or her discomfort; from saddling, bridling, mounting, and being ridden. Most horses with back issues will walk along fine with rider mounted. When you ask for increased forward motion, is when it'll show the most. Did he or she pin her ears, raise her neck and head? Has she or he shortened their stride?

Pay attention to all of this, and react accordingly. Most often the horse might just need a day or two off; a warm bath with an alcohol rinse does wonders for muscle soreness. Observe your horse when it is turned out. And again, react accordingly. If a horse that normally loves to roll and roll and roll, and now won't even roll once, is cause for concern. Know your horse and listen to what he or she is saying. Their actions speak volumes.

Horse Whisperers and Those Who talk a Little Too Loud

The reference isn't about the gentle hand laid upon a horse, a respectfulness of space or tactical repetition or the practice of taking one's time with a horse. It's not about the horseperson who cares and truly loves horses. It's about the so-called trainers who think force is a professional right. It's about the show offs, the know-it-alls, and the no-goods.

It is not acceptable to ever beat a horse under any circumstances. It's not acceptable to grab hold of the reins, pull hard on the bit, and start wailing on the horse's gut from the ground. It's not acceptable to whip a horse mercilessly over a jump. It is not acceptable to utter the words, "I'll show you who's boss." It is not acceptable. It is not admirable. It is not professional. The only thing that person is showing, is ignorance. If force is all this type of trainer has to offer, he or she needs to embark on another profession.

Horses can be stubborn, a horse can be dangerous. The fact that a horse can adapt so well to being domesticated, exemplifies their greatness, and their kindness. They are strong animals, they are intelligent, and for the most part, they are trusting. Gone are the days when a horse has to be broke – aka - "broken." I'm not sure who the original "Horse Whisperer" was or is. Many have staked claim to that title. But whoever it is or they are, I take my hat off to them. They have shed a different light on horsemanship forever.

Thank you to the person that pioneered watching a horse's body language. Not just a stomp of their foot or the tossing of the head, rearing, bucking and kicking. Just about anyone can figure out what those actions mean. They are loud and clear. It's the licking and the chewing, and the welcoming action of the horse's lowering his or her head. It's the look in their eye that says I trust you, the blinking, the softness, the conversation. The full body language that says, "Yes, I'd rather be standing over there next to you than over here by myself. Yes. We can do this. I'm listening." Give your horse a hug. A hug is the best form of horse whispering. It doesn't take talent, know how, or even a certain skill level. It's comes from the heart.

We hope you have enjoyed For the Love of Horses! We'd appreciate hearing from you, either through our website www.sunrisehorsefarm.com or with a review on www.amazon.com Thank you!!

Sunrise HORSE FARM

www.ingramcontent.com/pod-product-compliance
Lightning Source LLC
Chambersburg PA
CBHW070549030426
42337CB00016B/2415